habnf

158 FALL

W9-AEH-665

Faller, Heike
Hundred
33410016478911   10/27/19

Hebron Public Library
201 W. Sigler Street
Hebron, IN 46341

Heike Faller / Valerio Vidali

HUNDRED

WHAT YOU LEARN IN A LIFETIME

CELADON
BOOKS

NEW YORK

HUNDRED. Copyright © 2017 by Kein & Aber AG Zurich—Berlin. All rights reserved. English translation by Guenther A. Krumminga and Ruth Ahmedzai Kemp. Printed in China. For information, address Celadon Books, 120 Broadway, New York, NY 10271.

www.celadonbooks.com

Cover design and illustrations by Valerio Vidali

ISBN 978-1-250-23702-6 (hardcover)
ISBN 978-1-250-23701-9 (ebook)

Our books may be purchased in bulk for promotional, educational, or business use. Please contact your local bookseller or the Macmillan Corporate and Premium Sales Department at 1-800-221-7945, extension 5442, or by email at MacmillanSpecialMarkets@macmillan.com.

Originally published in Germany in 2018 under the title *Hundert* by Kein & Aber

First U.S. Edition October 2019

10 9 8 7 6 5 4 3 2 1

O
YOU SMILE FOR THE FIRST TIME IN YOUR LIFE.
AND OTHER PEOPLE SMILE BACK AT YOU!

$^1/_2$

EVERYTHING WITHIN REACH IS YOURS TO GRAB.

1
BUT IF YOU LET SOMETHING GO,
IT FALLS DOWN. YOU'VE DISCOVERED
GRAVITY.

1^1/$_2$
YOUR MOTHER SOMETIMES VANISHES,
BUT SHE ALWAYS COMES BACK AGAIN.
THIS IS CALLED TRUST.

2
YOU CAN DO A SOMERSAULT! WELL, NEARLY.

IT'S GOOD TO BE ALIVE...

3

... BUT BEING ALIVE ALSO MEANS DYING ONE DAY.

4
NEVER MIND THAT.
YOU FOCUS ON THE HERE AND NOW.

$4^3/_4$

SO MANY FLAVORS! WHICH ONES DO YOU LIKE?

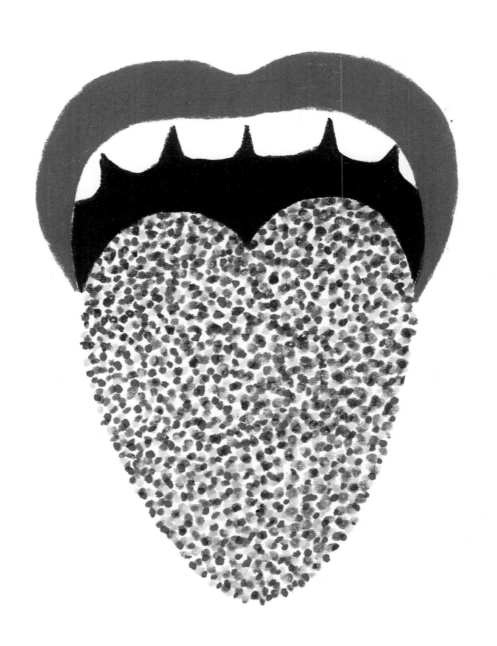

5
PEOPLE SAY GIRLS AND BOYS FALL IN LOVE.
NO WAY!

6
YOU'RE A BIG KID NOW,
GOING OFF TO SCHOOL WITH YOUR FRIENDS.

Aa   Bb   Cc

Dd   Ee   Ff

Gg   Hh   Ii

Ll   Mm   Nn

Oo   Pp   Qq

Rr   Ss   Tt

Uu   Vv   Zz

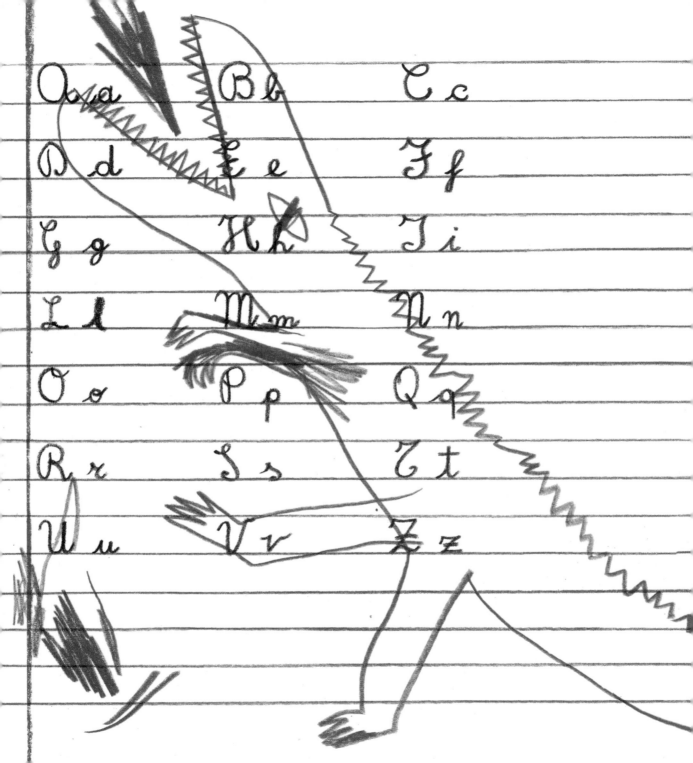

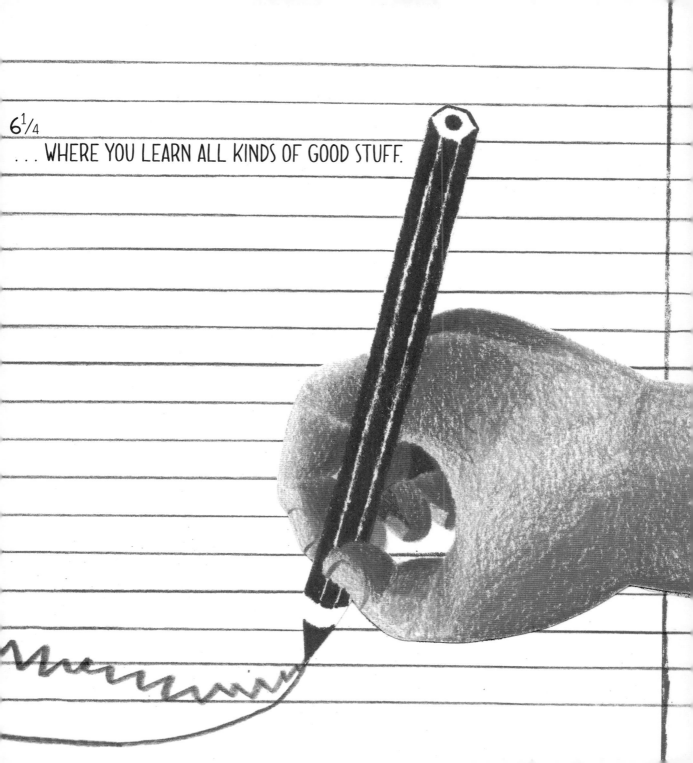

7
THE WORLD IS FULL OF THINGS TO DISCOVER.
EVERYTHING DESERVES CLOSE INSPECTION.

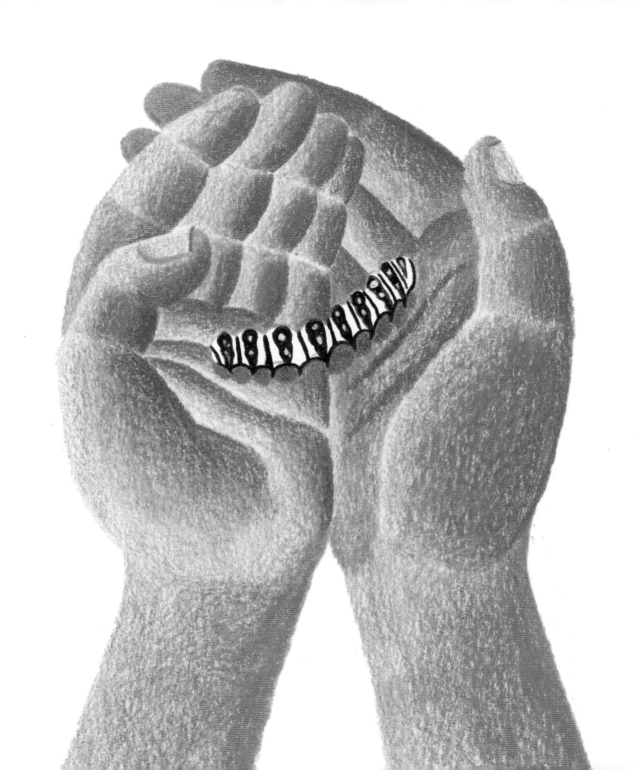

$7^1/_4$
BUT THEN SOMETIMES YOU GET SO BORED.

8
YOU GET BRAVER WITH
EVERY STEP YOU TAKE.

$8^1/_2$
. . . BUT ALSO MORE SKEPTICAL.

9
AMERICA. ITALY. BERLIN. SHERWOOD FOREST.
CORNWALL. THE MEDITERRANEAN. MOUNT EVEREST.
THE NORTH POLE. RUSSIA. AUSTRALIA.
THE WORLD IS GIGANTIC AND AMAZING!

10
BUT PEOPLE ALSO ONCE BUILT A PLACE CALLED
AUSCHWITZ.

11
DID YOU KNOW THAT SOME FISH GO BACK TO WHERE
THEY WERE BORN TO LAY THEIR EGGS?

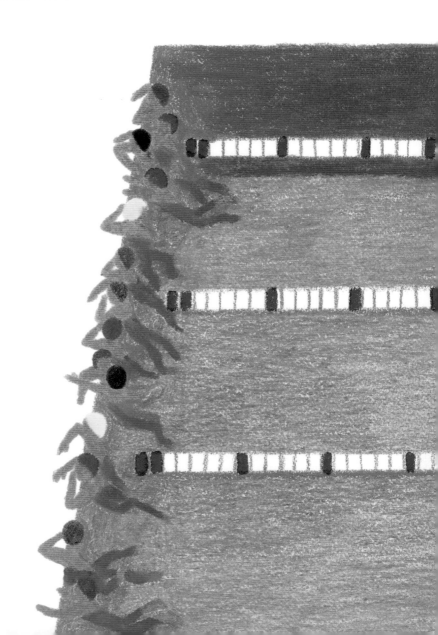

12
THERE'S TONS OF STUFF YOU'RE BETTER
AT THAN YOUR PARENTS.

13
BUT WHEN WILL THEY LEARN NOT TO CALL YOU
"BUNNY" IN FRONT OF YOUR FRIENDS?

14
YOU LEARN HOW TO BE LIKE EVERYONE ELSE
(ALTHOUGH YOU CAN'T ALWAYS PULL IT OFF).

15
YOU HEAR THAT THE MOST DISTANT THING WE CAN SEE IS THE
ANDROMEDA GALAXY.
IT'S HEADING FOR OUR GALAXY, THE MILKY WAY,
AND IN ABOUT 4 BILLION YEARS IT'S GOING TO CRASH INTO US!

16
NEVER MIND THAT.
YOU'RE LEARNING TO KISS

17
THE IMPOSSIBLE HAS HAPPENED. YOU'VE FALLEN IN LOVE.

18
JUST AS IMPOSSIBLE TO BELIEVE,
YOU ACTUALLY LIKE COFFEE!

19
BUT YOU DON'T ALWAYS LIKE YOURSELF.
CAN YOU CHANGE INTO SOMEONE ELSE?

20
HARD TO BELIEVE YOU WERE ONCE FIFTEEN.
FIVE YEARS SEEMS LIKE FOREVER.

21
DID YOU REALLY GROW UP IN THIS TINY ROOM?

22
WHEN YOU HAVE A GOAL,
BREAK IT DOWN INTO SMALL STEPS.

23
FOR THE FIRST TIME,
YOU TELL SOMEONE EVERYTHING ABOUT YOURSELF.

24
YOU'VE NEVER BEEN SO CLOSE TO ANYONE.

25
YOU'LL BE TOGETHER FOREVER

26

. . . OR MAYBE NOT.

27
YOUR MOTHER'S ADVICE ISN'T MUCH HELP.

28
BUT IT DOES COME WITH A JAR OF
HOMEMADE BLACKBERRY JAM.

29
THINGS YOU'VE YET TO LEARN:
HOW TO NOT FEEL DOWN ABOUT A QUIET
SATURDAY NIGHT AT HOME.

30
YOU START TO REALIZE THAT HAPPINESS IS RELATIVE.

31
IT COMES WHEN YOU'RE NOT REALLY
LOOKING FOR IT.

32

WHAT ABOUT CHILDREN?

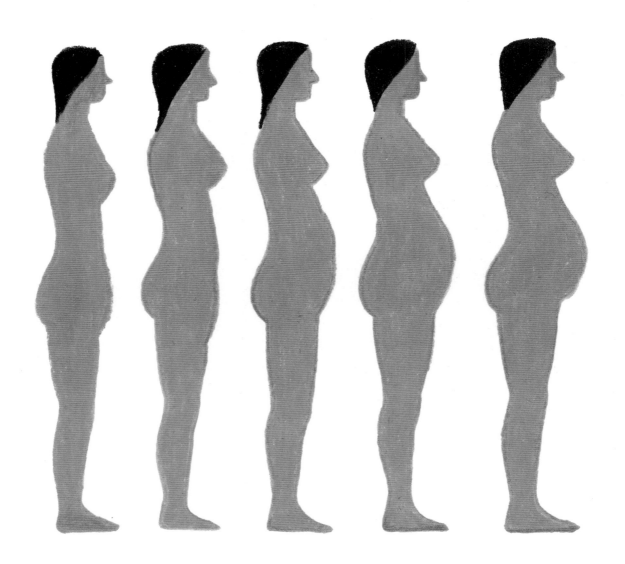

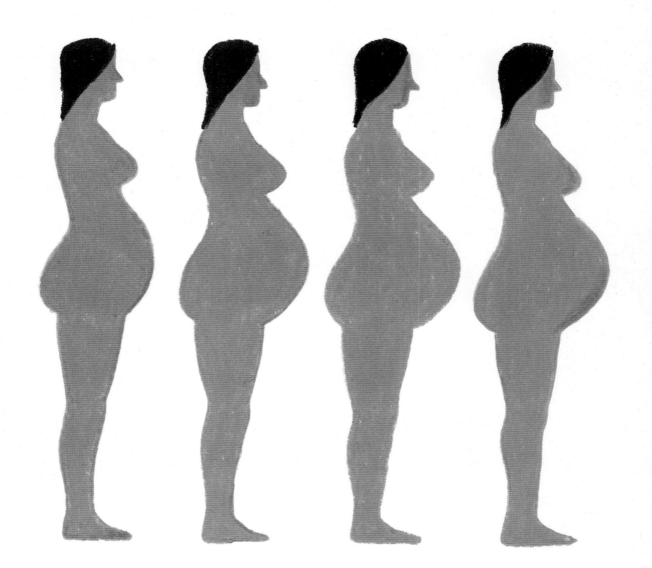

33
BETTER LEARN TO GET BY
WITHOUT SLEEP.

NOW YOU'RE DEFINITELY A GROWN-UP.

35
. . . OR MAYBE NOT.

36

IT'S A DREAM COME TRUE. BUT IT'S NOT EXACTLY
HOW YOU IMAGINED IT.

37
AT LEAST YOU CAN BE SILLY AGAIN!

38
IN NEW MEXICO THERE'S A PLACE CALLED
THE LIGHTNING FIELD
WHERE STEEL RODS ATTRACT LIGHTNING BOLTS FROM THE SKY.
THE WORLD IS STILL FULL OF SURPRISES.

39

YOU HAVE NEVER LOVED ANYONE SO MUCH . . .

40

... OR BEEN SO AFRAID FOR ANOTHER PERSON.

41
WHEN DID LIFE GET SO STRESSFUL?

42
AT LEAST YOU CAN MAKE YOUR OWN
BLACKBERRY JAM NOW.

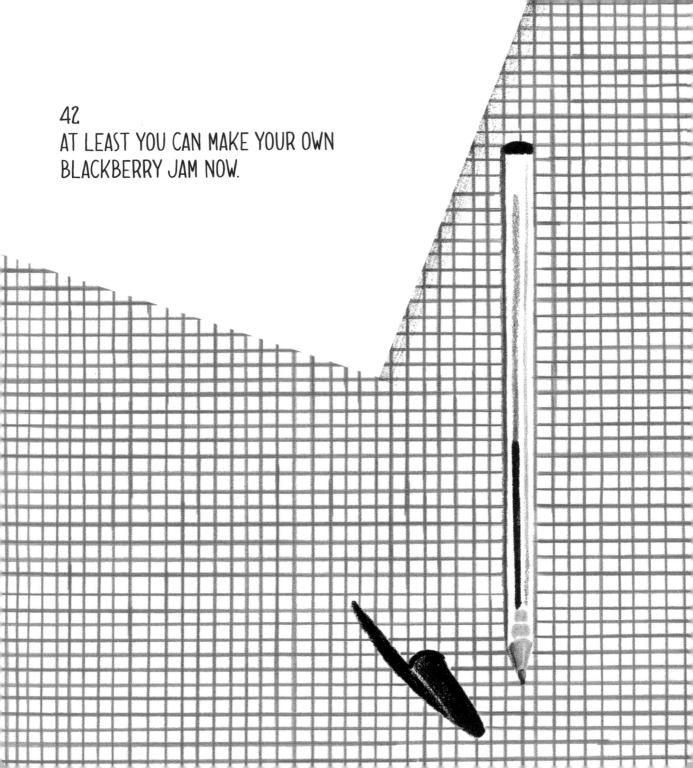

43
AND YOU'VE LEARNED TO BE COMFORTABLE
WITH BEING ALONE.

44
YOU HAVE WRINKLES ON YOUR TOES.

45
DO YOU LIKE YOURSELF THE WAY YOU ARE?

46
ARE YOU ONLY LEARNING NOW HOW IT FEELS TO LOSE SOMEONE?

47

48

THEN COUNT YOURSELF LUCKY.

49
YOU LEARN WHAT A LUXURY IT IS
TO SLEEP THROUGH THE NIGHT.

50
HIDDEN FORCES PULL US THIS WAY AND THAT.
WHICH IS THE STRONGEST?

51
YOU ACCEPT YOUR PARENTS AS THEY ARE.

52
YOU'RE STILL CHASING SOME OF YOUR DREAMS . . .

53
BUT THAT'S OK. YOU'VE LEARNED TO
APPRECIATE THE LITTLE THINGS...

54
... AND THE BIG THINGS.

55
TO APPRECIATE GRANDEUR, YOU NEED PERSPECTIVE.

56
YOU'VE GOTTEN USED TO THE WORLD.
SOMETIMES YOU DON'T EVEN NOTICE THE MOON.

57
IMAGINE IF IT ONLY APPEARED
EVERY HUNDRED YEARS.
THEN YOU'D NOTICE IT!

58
SOMETIMES IT'S HARD TO GET ALONG.

59

AND THE WORLD IS STILL STRANGE. DID YOU KNOW THAT SOME LAKES IN THE ALPS HAVE BELL TOWERS STICKING OUT OF THEM?

60
YOU'RE SIXTY NOW. AS A CHILD, SIXTY SEEMED
ANCIENT, BUT YOU HARDLY FEEL OLD AT ALL.

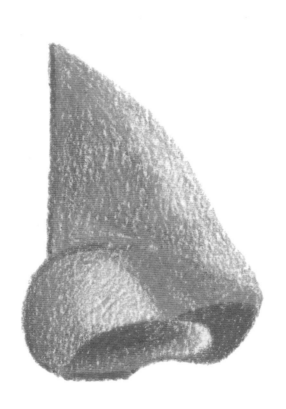

61
YOUR NOSE GETS BIGGER, AND SO DO YOUR EARS.

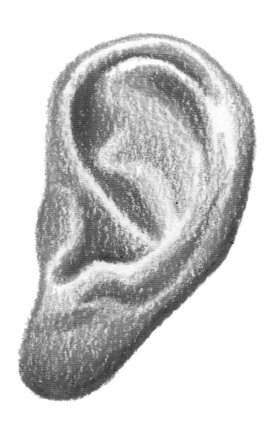

62
NO ONE THINKS OF THEMSELVES AS THE BAD GUY.

64
SOMETHING DRAWS YOU BACK TO WHERE YOU CAME FROM.

65
IS IT STILL HOME?

HI99

AX

67
MAYBE YOU'RE DISCOVERING THE WORLD.

68
MAYBE YOU'RE DISCOVERING YOUR GARDEN.

70
YOU STILL DON'T REALLY KNOW YOURSELF.
SOMETIMES YOU DON'T KNOW YOU LIKE SOMETHING
UNTIL YOU TRY IT.

71
SOME YEARS EVERYTHING IS HARD.

72

AND THERE ARE SOME WHERE LIFE IS EASY.

73
ARE THERE THINGS YOU WOULD HAVE DONE DIFFERENTLY?

74
FINALLY, PERHAPS, YOU FIND YOUR PERFECT MATCH.

75
SOME THINGS YOU LEARN, OTHERS YOU UNLEARN.
CAN YOU STILL DO A SOMERSAULT?

76
BEING IN NATURE IS THE BEST.

78
LET'S COME TO GRIPS WITH THIS NEW TECHNOLOGY.

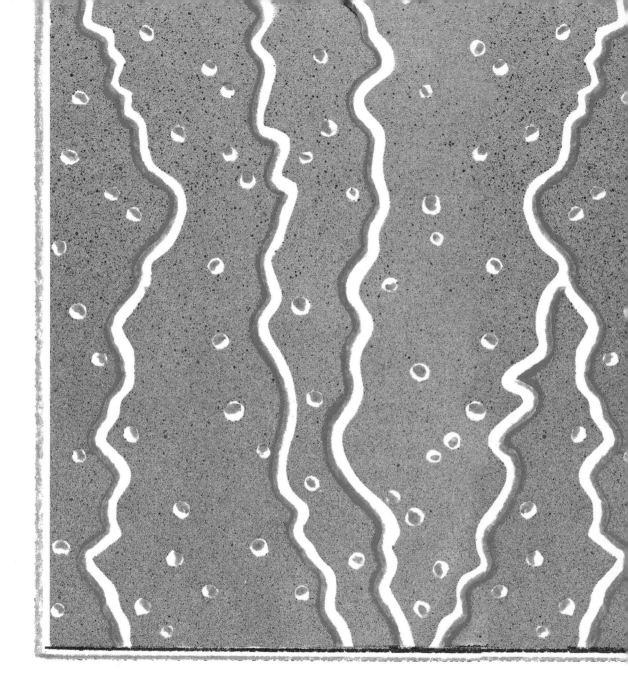

79
CAN YOU STILL DRIVE?

80
WHEN YOU KNOW THAT TIME IS FINITE,
YOU LIVE MORE IN THE PRESENT.

81
WHAT IF AGE WASN'T COUNTED IN YEARS,
BUT IN MOMENTS YOU'VE TREASURED?

82
EVERYTHING TAKES TWICE AS LONG.

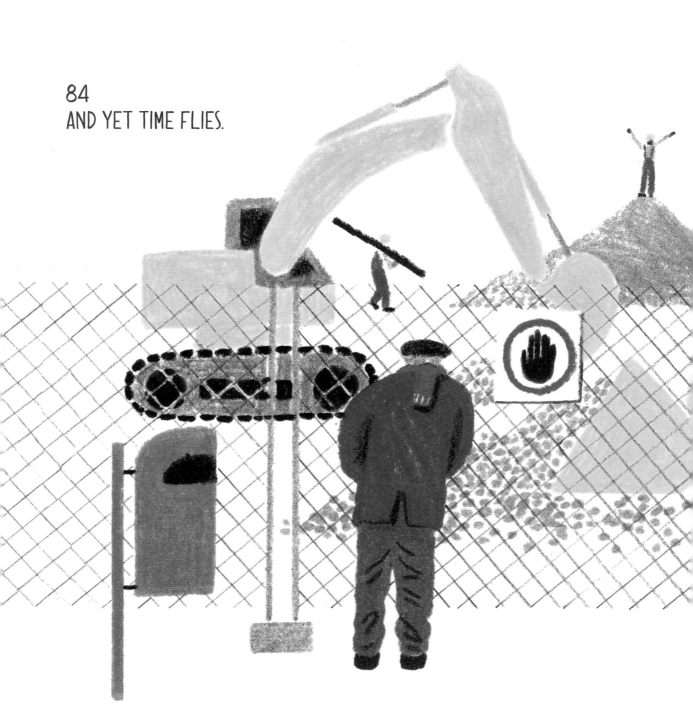

84
AND YET TIME FLIES.

86
THINGS CAN CHANGE FROM ONE MOMENT TO THE NEXT.

YOUR PARTNER'S HEALTH MIGHT GO DOWNHILL.

89
IT'S HARD.

90
LIFE HAS ITS UPS AND DOWNS.

91
IT FEELS GOOD TO HAVE AN OLD FRIEND TO RELY ON.

92
WHAT ABOUT DEATH? I SUPPOSE IT'LL COME ALONG.

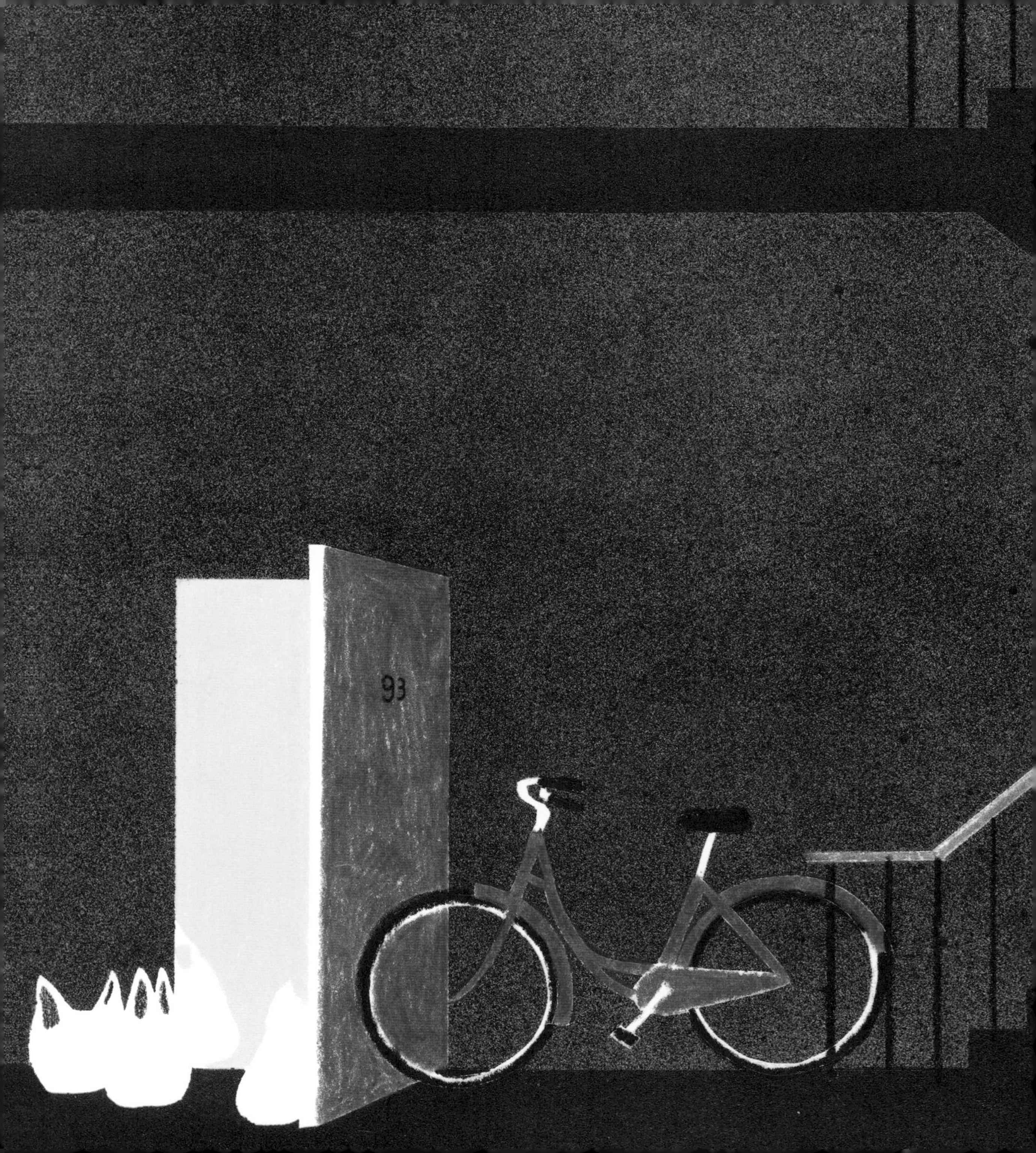
93

94
EVERY YEAR WHEN YOU PUT THE
EMPTY JAM JARS BACK IN THE CELLAR,
YOU WONDER IF YOU'RE GOING TO NEED
THEM ANYMORE.

95
AND THEN YOU MAKE YOUR BLACKBERRY JAM AGAIN.

96
AND BEFORE YOU KNOW IT, IT'S SPRING AGAIN.

PEOPLE ASK YOU ALL KINDS OF THINGS, LIKE:
WHAT HAS LIFE TAUGHT YOU?

YET SOMETIMES YOU FEEL LIKE THE CHILD
YOU ONCE WERE.

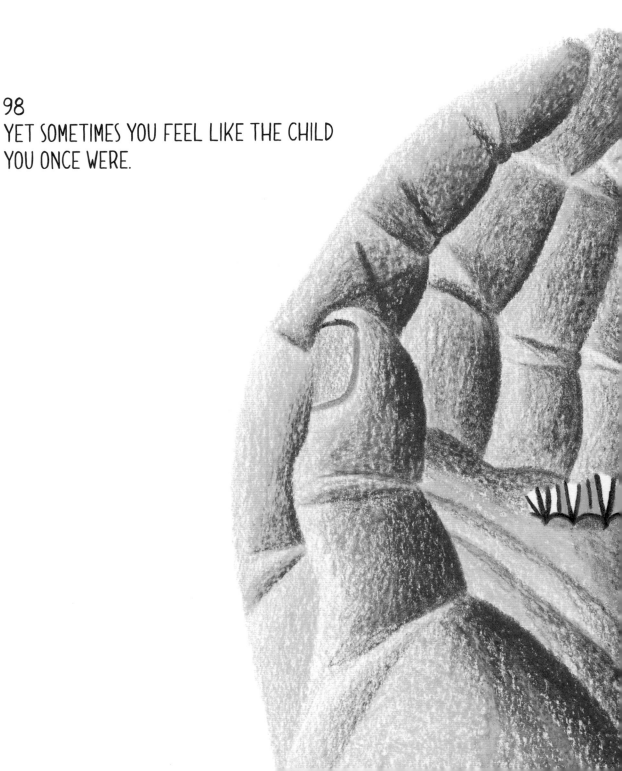

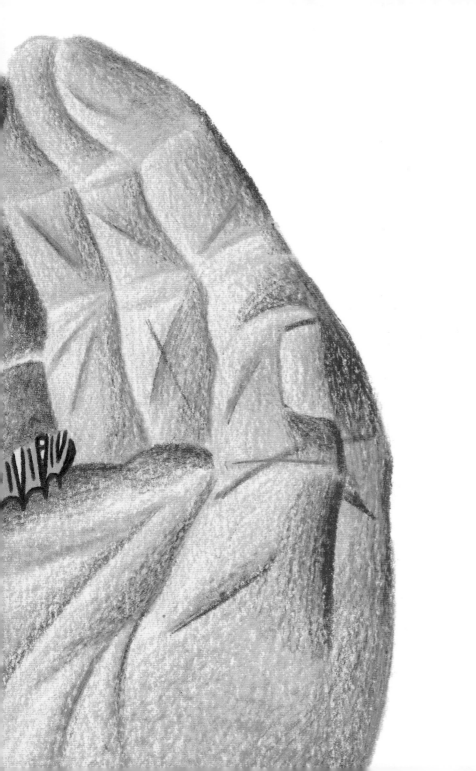

99
WHAT HAVE YOU LEARNED FROM LIFE?

The idea for this book . . .

. . . first came to me when I was looking at my newborn niece, wrapped up in her bed like a mummy and blinking into the world. What a strange journey awaits you, I thought. I half envied her for all the great things that lay ahead of her. But at the same time, I felt myself filled with sorrow as I thought of all the painful experiences that lay ahead of her as well.

At that moment a car drove by outside.

My niece moved her head, trying to follow the sound. She didn't yet understand that the noise had nothing to do with her own life.

When I saw her again a few weeks later, she was no longer reacting to car noises. She had by then begun the ongoing process of wondering, evaluating, and sorting out that enables us to avoid being overloaded with stimuli and, instead, move from A to B without picking up every pretty stone or jumping into every puddle along the way. Sadly, though, as grown-ups, we've become so accustomed to the world that even marvels like mountains, a full moon, or the love of another person become something we take for granted. And in order to see them again in their grandeur, we need to learn to see them with new eyes. That's what this book is all about: the way our perception of the world changes over the course of a lifetime.

There are many things that I have never—or, at least, have not yet—experienced. Which is why I decided to ask other people what they've learned in life. I talked to elementary school kids and ninety-year-olds; men and women who are much respected in our society as well as those who have lost their status. I sat with the former director-general of an East German company (Kombinat) in his garden in a village not far away from the high-rise buildings of Marzahn, a neighborhood in Berlin, and with a Syrian refugee family on the concrete floor of their basement apartment in Istanbul. The question I asked all these people was always the same: What have you learned in life?

A twenty-two-year-old from Lagos who had recently graduated high school talked about how he discovered the importance of planning out even the smallest steps needed to achieve something great. He had not done well in school, but once this insight came to him, he finished school with one of the highest grade-point averages in Nigeria.

People who had faced great hardships in their lives often said how surprised they were by their own strength. The Syrian mother of six, for example, whom I had encountered in Istanbul, told me she had discovered that though there really was no place for the poor in the world, life was beautiful, and one must try to be open to that beauty. Interestingly, it seemed that people who had encountered difficulties in life were often more easily satisfied than those who had traveled less treacherous paths. In this respect, perhaps life is fair after all: Happiness is relative (an idea touched upon in the pages of this book for ages 30 and 31).

Maybe this is why people are more grateful in their middle years, even for such simple delights as a delicious cappuccino enjoyed in a nice setting (at 51) or a good night's sleep (at 49). Actually, almost everyone over the age of 40 told me how happy they were when they were able to sleep through a night.

And the elderly? Of course, much of what one has learned by the time one has reached old age has to do with accepting limitations. But some people I interviewed also talked about totally new experiences. The East German director-general had concluded that he could have been braver. That's why, he said, he's now, at the age of 70, trying new things. A teacher from Upper Bavaria told me that at the age of 74, she finally found a partner who really suited her. And a painter from Berlin talked of when her husband started suffering from dementia. It was an extremely difficult time for her (see age 87), but one in which she also learned something new. Her husband's aides turned out to be working-class people of the sort that the couple had never had much contact with. But after spending time together, the painter discovered just how wise many of these aides were. And with that, her way of looking at people, the woman said, had changed completely in old age.

Yet despite all one's life experiences, there seems to be something within people that remains constant. This was brought home to me by my conversation with a ninety-four-year-old writer from London who had written a young adult book that is loved the world over. When I asked her what she had learned in life, she said, "Sometimes I feel like the little girl I used to be. I wonder if I have learned anything at all in life"—two sentences I've copied verbatim.

What surprised me most was that none of the older people I talked to feared death. The most beautiful expression of this came from a very old man who was with his wife when I visited them in their garden.

"Every year, when you bring the empty jam jars down to the cellar, you think: Who knows if you'll need them another time?" He paused. "But then you go back to preserve blackberry jam again."

This was the basis for ages 94 and 95 in the book (and the reason for the jam theme spread throughout).

There is, though, a problem with "life experience": It tends to ring hollow if you are unable to fill in the details with personal reflections. One way for readers to deal with this is to look at this book together with another person, someone—maybe a parent or grandparent—who has had more experiences, and to talk about what some of these sentences might have to do with his or her life. At least, that's what I hoped when I wrote this book.

—*Heike Faller*

About the Author

HEIKE FALLER is (probably) somewhere in the middle of her life. She is an editor at *Zeit Magazin* and dedicates this book to her nieces, Paula and Lotta, who—as babies—gave her the idea, and then kindly helped with the implementation a few years later.

About the Illustrator

VALERIO VIDALI is an Italian illustrator living in Berlin. He is younger than Heike, but older than Heike's nieces. His work has received many awards.